What Two Young Ladies Are Saying About
"Lessons to Share with the Daughter I Never Had"

Living in your 20's can be a complicated place. Everyday my mind does backflips in determining what's important. Relationships, employment, and experiences all seem like make or break situations. I can be safe or take risks. I can work hard or live freely. The rules developed by life decisions haven't been formed. I am unlimited in my choices, but bound by my willingness to discover myself. Like most, I didn't know where to start.

That's why this book inspires me. It gives young adults like myself a printed path to self-discovery. For most of us, it's a struggle just to find happiness. The bigger concerns: values, beliefs, and knowing yourself are often ignored. "It will take care of itself," is a common disclaimer. This book presents self-discovery as an active process -- not a passive happenstance.

Asking for help in figuring out what I wanted felt weird. How is someone else supposed to know me, better than me? This book will help. It is a resource that will narrow down my questions and help me concentrate on my foundation. It will allow me to discover the basics about what I consider important.

Also this book is spiritually based. I've been a follower of God my entire life. To have steps broken down, on a level that's complementary to the growth of my spirit, is comforting. I will be able to keep Him in the forefront of my mind while reading. In prayer, I thank Him every day for making me. I believe Him who created me, should lead me. No one knows better than God who I am, and what I'm meant to do.

Altogether, I'm very grateful for this book. It will help me, and I know it can help others. No one's path into adulthood is the same, but everyone can learn more about themselves. Who knows, you might discover someone you really like!

Deriah Groomes, *Linda's Niece*

After reading the 1st chapter, I learned so much on the importance of values and what my values really were compared to what I thought they were. The line that stood out the most was “Values act as a personal compass; they give us direction.” In that moment it all became clear on why knowing and understanding my values are vital for me to understand before I can understand my purpose, because my purpose is based around my values. This book has helped me understand that I can have a short-term purpose, since my purpose may change throughout my life.

Hearing Linda’s story on discovering her purpose provided encouragement for me. I see that I am not the only young lady confused about life’s choices, and now I have a guide to help me sort through the noise of life and bring some order along the way. I have enjoyed discovering more about myself with each turn of the page. I will use the information I have gained from this book to confidently make value-based choices, to ensure that my life continues in the direction of what I value most. This was such an easy read, I loved the mix of expository and descriptive writing style, great way to break up some of the heaviness self-help books can bring.

Velvet Hoskins
Achieving My Purpose (AMP) mentee & advisor

Lessons

TO SHARE WITH THE DAUGHTER I NEVER HAD

Linda G. Walton

www.LessonsToShareBook.com

For more information regarding special discounts for bulk purchases, please contact Linda Walton
lwalton@acheivingmypurpose.org
ISBN-13: 978-1503308978 *Paperback*
ISBN-10: 1503308979

Dedication

To the special young ladies in my life who inspired me to write this book: my niece, Deriah, my goddaughter, RaChelle, my three stepdaughters Alexis, Chanell and Melanie and to all young ladies everywhere.

Table of Contents

Acknowledgements

There are so many who deserve thanks for helping me complete this book, starting with my Heavenly Father who put it on my heart to embark on this journey at this time and place and the strength to see it through.

To my husband, James Walton, who has sacrificed some of our quality time to give me the time and space I needed to complete this project. A special thanks for your love, support, and especially the prayers as I travelled through this journey.

To my mom who shared her unconditional love and insight when she provided "the daughter she did have" with my early lessons. I must say, mom, you have been an amazing role model who has blazed a wonderful path for me to follow, and I honor and appreciate you for it.

To my friend, Kyra, who knew I was supposed to birth a book long before I knew myself. Thank you for the many years of encouragement.

To my friend, Marquetta, who cultivated my writing by gifting me with several beautiful journals and so many inspirational books.

To Joel, my coach and accountability partner who always had the right words to keep me going when I didn't think I could. You instilled in me that I was a "positively powerful woman" destined for greatness.

To my soror, my friend, Connie, who I owe a great deal of gratitude for lending her expertise to this project. You generously provided technical and moral support throughout the time I was writing this manuscript. This book could not have happened without your assistance. Words cannot express how much I appreciate you.

To Suzanne, Kim, Shawn, and Victoria who were the "wind beneath my wings". Ladies, you shared in my vision for this book and provided me support, encouragement, and prayers that motivated me to keep working to make this book a reality.

To my spiritual leader, Bishop Alexis Thomas who inspired me with his vision of the house which was "We are Walking Examples of Liberated Lives" and "This is the Year that We See it." I embraced your theme and it happened; thank you! To First Lady Michele Thomas, thank you for inviting me to work with the young women's ministry.

To the young ladies of LEED (Ladies Empowered to Embrace Destiny), the young women's ministry of Pilgrim Rest Baptist Church, thank you for your inspiration and allowing me to test some of my principles on you.

To Rick Forgus, the graphic designer who took my concept for the book cover and breathed life into it. I thank you for such great work.

To my sorors of Alpha Kappa Alpha Sorority, Inc., my sisters of the Links, and all the other wonderful women that I have been blessed to be affiliated with, I thank you because my life has been enriched by our connections.

Lastly, I thank all my loving family and friends who have molded me and contributed to the woman I have become. I thank God for allowing you to be a part of my life and the role you have played in my success.

Foreword

by Dr. Freddie Groomes-McLendon
F. Lang Groomes Associates

"Lessons to Share With the Daughter I Never Had" is a most intriguing title. However this foreword is being penned by the mother of the author. I am so very proud of Linda and am pleased and proud to offer this foreword. I frequently refer to her as my favorite daughter when she is actually my only daughter. I also had one son, the late Derek Ramone'. Linda was always special perhaps because she was my first born and was actually conceived on my honeymoon with the love of my life, *(Something very few people knew until now).*

This book is so very timely at this point in history. There are so many young people in dire need of advice or counseling as they attempt to navigate through the challenges and opportunities before them. Many parents are ill-equipped to address the unique needs confronting their children in this new era. Too many of the parents are young and inexperienced with the traditional demands of parenting. Thus, the merit and tremendous value of this publication.

Effective parenting involves loving care and efficient supportive provisions for children. These can be provided by the parents or other family members, friends or "the community," but it must be provided if a child is to thrive and not just survive. Effective parenting is especially critical for young women, which is why Linda is right on focus as she addresses the topics in her book. This book could very easily have been called *"Strategies For Success in Life"* because it addresses the salient issues that confront young women.

Success is personal and is the result of deliberate effort. The characteristics of success for one is not exactly the same for another, but I believe significant success requires determination, dedication, positive self-concept, positive values, and commitment to the realization of success. The person must be well rounded and possess the qualities that society demands. The demands of society are many and diverse but they are indeed expected and often mandated. Young women must have these qualities, or be able to acquire them. This book explains the major requirements and expectations in a potent manner.

This book offers a road map to accomplishments, beginning with the need to determine or define one's purpose. Why we are here and what purpose do we serve? This may seem a simple query to some but to clearly define one's purpose is no easy task. Often mentors can be vital to this process. This book affords many options as well as questions that, when answered, will provide substance to define one's purpose. This book provides supportive scriptures for all of its chapters, which serves as an unmatchable resource for the reader.

Once we have defined our purpose, there is a

tremendous responsibility to consider our personal values. What do I represent in life as a member of the larger society? How am I perceived by others as I demonstrate my values from day to day and situation to situation? Are my values such that I am proud of them and do they serve me well as I define my purpose? As the author beautifully states, "[your] values act as a personal compass." A compass charts direction and so do your values. Your value system can chart a course of success or destruction. This book provides a systematic approach and raises serious and pointed questions that are practical in assisting you with the task of defining your values.

Clearly, this book provides the tools to aid you in finding your purpose or helping you to more accurately articulate your purpose. When this has been successfully realized you will be poised to travel the road ahead and meet the challenges and opportunities that are before you. With positive personal values, you are equipped to manage effectively whatever life offers. Nothing is to say that your life will be obstacle free, but I do believe that when properly equipped as this book proposes, your response to whatever happens will be conquerable.

This book is a tremendous contribution to the reader who is interested in the good life as God wills it. I hope that the reader will adhere to the wisdom of its contents and thus be better prepared as this author has intended. Life is what you make it; a good definition of purpose and a positive value system are wonderful beginnings for the good life and success.

With that, I hasten to add the critical importance that the book places on spiritual and mental health. As a Christian woman I know that God has blessed me and protected me in innumerous ways, and I could have never made this life journey without Him. I offer my personal testimony: "Having been born some X number of years ago to Negro parents living in a Colored community, and attending separate but equal schools, life for me ain't been no crystal stair. It's been laced with many challenges and opportunities. but I have more than survived, I have thrived as a proud African American woman". Thank you Jesus. If I dare to say, I believe you must have faith and believe in a power greater than yourself.

I believe that your body is your temple and it must be taken care of. The book addresses our need for physical and emotional health and suggests strategies for the same. The mind and the body works in concert, and this publication addresses strategies to assist you as you wage war on temptation and achieve good mental and physical health.

The book addresses the matter of financial health and economic empowerment. What is a successful life without the comforts of well-being? Here you find well organized strategies that address earning financial resources and how to effectively manage them for financial health. Further, the book suggests how you may utilize your financial accomplishments to give you a positive base for ultimate economic empowerment.

I think my favorite daughter has done a marvelous job with this her first publication in addressing vital issues that confront young people and especially young women. It contains a special recipe that when all the ingredients are included, and properly mixed, will yield a most successful product.

Like any mother, I am so proud of my daughter. Although my daughter's title refers to daughters she never had, I do not doubt that Linda will accumulate a retinue of "daughters" and even "sons", who may be impacted by this inspiring and instructional manuscript.

I can imagine that this will be a best seller, because the recipe for success that Linda shares works and I know it firsthand. How so?

They are the same principles Linda has used in her own life and with great success. She was one of the first female executives at a Fortune 500 company back in the 80's. She has enjoyed significant appointments at both the state and national levels. Recently, Alpha Kappa Alpha Sorority, Inc., the oldest and largest African American Sorority, appointed Linda as its Chairman of Leadership

Training. Although I am unashamedly biased, I know that my daughter is well-equipped to provide insightful and inspiring instruction because she has personified the values espoused in this book as a professional, as a wife, community leader and certainly as a daughter and a woman of God.

Introduction

I am writing this book to inspire young ladies to recognize that each of them has a purpose, for them to discover that purpose, and to embrace pathways that lead them to their destiny. You may be asking yourself, "Why another book about things I already know?" When I used to see books similar to this one, I'd ask the same question. The answer is -- I am sharing from my experiences and from my perspective. So there is your answer. I hope you will be curious enough to keep reading.

If you are anything like I am, sometimes you think you know it all. Nobody can tell you anything. Even though we were told that "the stove is hot," we had to touch it anyway.

Just like with me, some of this advice might fall on deaf ears. Growing up, I thought I knew more than the wise women before me. Or I felt, they lived in the dark ages; life is different now. I have since learned there is really nothing new under the sun, although it might be dressed up a little differently.

I have paid the price for my hard head. Unfortunately for me, some life lessons, I chose to learn through personal trials. There were wonderful people in my life who have tried to impart wisdom: my mother, aunts, grandparents, etc. Thank God I had enough sense to listen to *most* of it! And, I must say, I have been truly blessed. Some young ladies are not blessed to have people in their lives to share little nuggets with them -- no fault of their own. Some of you may find yourselves in the same situation.

I must confess, if I had listened more I could have saved myself some battle scars. A word of caution: What I am sharing is not the path I have always taken; much of what you will read is what I should have done! As you journey along life's pathways, you will make mistakes, because none of us is perfect! Hopefully, if you take heed to some of the advice given in this book, you won't make the same mistakes I made.

Over the years, I have shared my personal life

lessons with young girls and women who have crossed my path: my niece, goddaughter, stepdaughters, mentees, etc. Yet there are so many more young people that I may not be able to touch personally. It is my desire through this writing that I will be able to touch many more wonderful lives.

I hope you will enjoy reading, nibble on the nuggets, and walk away from this reading experience more empowered. Finally, if the lessons work for you, "Pay it Forward," and share with young ladies who are willing and need to listen to your story!

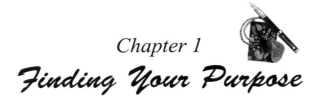

Chapter 1
Finding Your Purpose

"For I know the plans I have for you," declares the Lord, "plans to prosper you and not to harm you, plans to give you hope and a future."

Jeremiah 29:11 NIV

"The purpose of life is a life of purpose"
~ Robert Byrne

For each of us, there is a beginning (a check-in date) and an ending (a check-out date) on this earth. The check-out date is the appointment that will not be cancelled. Given that fact, we need to focus on the time in between. What will be your life story?

Finding your purpose is one of the most – if not *the* most – important decisions you will make during your life's journey! To determine your purpose, ask yourself: What do I want to do with my life that will matter to me? Will my decision have meaning for anyone other than me? Does it have to? In addition, purpose focuses on why: Why do I want to do *this* rather than *that*? Without purpose, you will find yourself wandering, drifting, and going nowhere fast!

Your purpose may manifest itself in different ways over your life span. At your young age, it might be answered through questions such as:

"What do I want to be when I grow up?
"Who do I admire so much that I want to be like him/her?
"What are my favorite subjects in school? (Then exploring careers related to those subjects.)
"What do I enjoy doing when I am not in school?"

As you get older, perhaps as a young adult, another way that might help you determine your life's direction is to take a personal or career assessment which might offer suggestions. Of course, don't underestimate the importance of asking family members and close friends to offer their opinions based on their observations of your personality and interests. How can this help? It just might validate and confirm the direction that you had been hearing all along from that small, soft, inner voice in your spirit. I want to be clear: Having a defined purpose does not guarantee you will achieve it, but not having a purpose at all makes the journey more difficult!

God created each of us for a purpose when He breathed life into each of us through our mothers and fathers. As such, it was no mistake in your being born. God knew before your parents even met what was going to happen. For those of you who were born out of wedlock, there are no illegitimate children. God brought you on this earth for a purpose. The key is finding your purpose and pursuing it.

As you journey down a path that you feel the Lord is leading you, do understand it may change several times along the way. In my teenage years, I vacillated between wanting to be a medical doctor to being an engineer. However, after I had taken a battery of tests in school, the results reflected that I had a strong inclination towards numbers and analyses. The career assessment identified the occupations of many of the individuals in my "circle of life" that I was attracted to and influenced by.

My results were further supported by family members and friends. I was challenged by the fact that professions that required math, chemistry, and other sciences, were not heavily populated by women. I was starting to believe part of my purpose was doing things fairly nontraditional and out of the ordinary. I liked the challenge of charting down a course that was less travelled. I was encouraged by very supportive parents who instilled in me the thought that I could do anything I made up my mind to do. This lesson will be discussed in a future chapter focusing on supportive relationships.

Finding your ultimate purpose in life will probably not be totally defined in your younger years. However, you may be able to identify a short-term purpose for now. Developing the basics for this life's journey is a reasonable goal.

One aspect of finding your purpose is defining or identifying your values -- what you believe in—that internal compass!

Values

When I talk about establishing your personal values, I am encouraging you to ask yourself what you want to stand for. What are those things that I truly believe in? Values are priorities that tell you how you want to spend your time; they define what is really most important to you.

When you discover what those values are, it is much easier to commit to decisions and actions that support them and are less complex. When you think of a value, think of a quality that makes something desirable or undesirable.

If you know someone's values, you can predict their behavior. When your actions start becoming contradictory, things don't seem to be going right. It might be because some parts of your life are not in alignment with your values.

Values act as personal compasses; they give us direction. Though values are relatively stable, our focus on a particular value may shift from time to time. Most certainly, the order of priority of your values are sure to change over time. For example, as your definition of success changes, so do your values. I offer a list of values, just to help you create a stronger sense of what is most important to you. While it is certainly not an all-inclusive list, there are lots of sources I will recommend for you to explore and identify the ones that best fit for you.

Defining Your Values

According to *Mind Tools*, a training organization, a good way to define your values is to look back over your life (no matter how old you are) – to identify when you felt good and really confident that you were making good choices. The following is a model that *Mind Tools* used to ascertain what matters most to you:

Step 1: Identify the times when you were happiest

Find examples from your school, work, and personal life as this will ensure some balance in your answers.

- What were you doing?
- Were you with other people? Who?
- What other factors contributed to your happiness?

Step 2: Identify the times when you were most proud

Use examples from your career and personal life.

- Why were you proud?
- Did other people share your pride? Who?
- What other factors contributed to your feelings of pride?

Step 3: Identify the times when you were most fulfilled and satisfied

Again, use school, work, or personal examples.

- What need or desire was fulfilled?
- How and why did the experience give your life meaning?
- What other factors contributed to your feelings of fulfillment?

Step 4: Determine your top values, based on your

experiences of happiness, pride, and fulfillment

Why is each experience truly important and memorable? Use the following list of common personal values to help you get started. Aim to choose approximately 10 top values. As you work through, you may find that some of these naturally combine. For instance, if you value philanthropy, community, and generosity, you might say that service to others is one of your top values.

Alphabetical List of Values (from *Mind Tools* – Essentials Skills for an Excellent Career)

- Accomplishment
- Ambition
- Being the best
- Caring
- Change
- Commitment
- Confidence
- Dependability
- Discipline
- Education
- Ethics
- Excellence
- Fairness
- Faith
- Family
- Financial Independence
- Freedom
- Friendship
- Giving
- Gratitude
- Guidance
- Happiness
- Health
- Honesty
- Humility
- Humor
- Individuality
- Integrity
- Intelligence
- Joy
- Kindness
- Knowledge
- Leadership
- Love
- Making a Difference
- Marriage
- Optimism
- Organization
- Peace
- Power
- Relaxation
- Respect
- Responsibility
- Self-Control
- Self-Respect
- Spirituality
- Spontaneity
- Strength
- Success
- Thoughtfulness
- Tradition
- Truth
- Uniqueness
- Vision

The following are several words or phrases that describe some of my personal values and what they mean to me:

Faith - I do believe that God is the head of my life, and I sincerely believe He directs my path. This leads me to treat others by the Golden Rule, "Do unto others as you would have them do unto you." (Luke 6:31 NIV)

Compassion – If I can help somebody along the way, then my living will not be in vain.

Excellence – Do everything to the best of my ability.

Security – Safety is still a basic need. I am not willing to take unnecessary risks.

Continuous Learning – Never stop having the desire to learn.

Friendships - I truly enjoy connecting with friends and family.

Success, Achievement, Accomplishment – Serve as "motivators" for me.

Family – My relationship with my family is important.

Step 5: Prioritize Your Top Values

This step is probably the most difficult, because you'll have to look deep inside yourself. It's also the most important step, because, when making a decision, you'll have to choose between solutions that may satisfy different values. This is when you must know which value is more important to you.

• Write down your top values, not in any particular order.

• Look at the first two values and ask yourself, "If I could satisfy only one of these, which would I choose?" It might help to visualize a situation in which you would have to make that choice. For example, if you compare the values of service and stability, imagine that you must decide whether to sell your house and move to another country to do valuable foreign aid work, or keep your house and volunteer to do charity work closer to home.

• Keep working through the list, by comparing each value, until your list is in the order that fits YOU!

Step 6: Reaffirm your values

Check your top-priority values, and make sure they fit you and your vision for your life.

• Do these values make you feel good about yourself?

• Are you proud of your top three values?

• Would you be comfortable and proud to tell your values to people you respect and admire?

• Do these values represent things you would support, even if your choice isn't popular, and it puts you in the minority?

Making value-based choices may not always be easy. However, making a choice that you know is right is a lot less difficult in the long run. Identifying and understanding your values is a challenging and important exercise. Your values are a central part of who you are – and who you want to be. By becoming more aware of these important factors in your life, you can use them as a guide to make the best choice in any situation.

When your values, passion, and gifts intersect, you will know your purpose. Your human compass will guide you down the road to discovery. You will know that you are on the right course. Your path will just feel right!

Goals

"What you get by achieving your goals is not as important as what you become by achieving your goals." ~ **Henry David Thoreau**

Once you have determined the values you live by, it's time to create the plan for your life in terms of goals. Goals are experiences you shoot for that will make you feel good about your life. Goal setting is a process for thinking about your future. Having a goal will help you organize your time and talent so it can be the most fulfilled. Goals help you with saying, "no." It's a lot easier to say "no" to a request that will not support achieving your individual goals.

The most powerful goals are SMART ones: Specific, Measurable, Achievable, Relevant and

Timely[2]. Consider establishing goals in the areas of career, education, financial, spiritual, and health and wellness. Once the goals have been established, share them with a trusted confidante who will help you stay accountable. The following is an example of a set of goals I have personally established. This is a fluid list - it is subject to change once you have accomplished the goal(s) or it (they) no longer meet the SMART test.

Career/professional – to launch a successful nonprofit organization in the next 12 months

Educational – to obtain a doctorate degree in 3 years

Financial – to acquire financial wealth and investment income in 2 years

Travel – to take a vacation aboard or within the USA annually

Self-Confidence

Once you have determined your values and goals, the next key thing is to have a good dose of self-confidence that will allow you to achieve anything. Self-confidence is the ability to be certain about your character and your capabilities. You have to feel good about yourself, or fake it until you do.

There's an old adage which states, "sticks and stones may break your bones, but words will never hurt you." Not true! Words hurt! They hurt at the core of who you are, if you don't have a healthy dose of self-confidence or self-esteem.

So how do you develop positive self-esteem?

1. You have to know that you are loved unconditionally.
2. You have to believe in yourself and build your own character and competence in your skills and talents.
3. Learn to love yourself with your flaws.
4. Do what you believe is right, even if you are criticized for it.
5. Make mistakes, admit them and learn from them.

Now, the opposite of positive self-esteem is negative self-esteem. If you don't feel good about yourself, it could make you sick or depressed. How do you turn this around? The answer is to think and act differently.

1. Use positive affirmations to encourage yourself.
2. Meditate and let God talk to you.
3. Identify role models to emulate.
4. Don't rely completely on the words of others for your self-confidence. Those who build you up may also tear you down because of jealousy, envy or their own lack of confidence.
5. Strive to be the best you can be!

God has given us everything we need to succeed. But even with that, sometimes bad things happen to good people. Remember, God doesn't give us anything that we can't handle as long as we look to Him for guidance. He knows what is going to happen before it happens! Whether you are faced with the death of a loved one, divorce from your spouse or loss of a job, you can overcome with God! Don't be "hung up" about what people say when they talk negatively about you. It is often more a reflection of how they feel about themselves.

Words of Wisdom:

"Keep your thoughts positive because your thoughts become your words.

Keep your words positive because your words become your behavior.

Keep your behavior positive because your behavior becomes your habits.

Keep your habits positive because your habits become your values.

Keep your values positive because your values become your destiny."

~Mahatma Ghandi

Reflections/Plan of Action

"I want us all to fulfill our greatest potential. To find our calling, and summon the courage to live it." ~ ***Oprah***

- ✓ What is my passion? What do I enjoy doing most?

  ____

  ____

- ✓ What would I work hard at even without pay?

  ____

  ____

- ✓ What will be my primary focus at (age) to help achieve or realize my purpose?

  18 years old

  ____

  30 years old

  ____

  40 years old

  ____

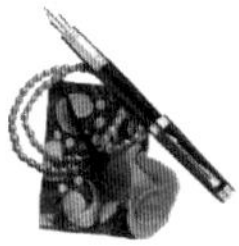

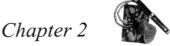

Chapter 2
Developing and Maintaining Relationships

"A new commandment I give to you, that you love one another: as I have loved you, that you also love one another."

John 13:34 NKJV

"Love isn't when there are no fights in the relationship. Love is when once the fight ends, love is still there."

- ***Author Unknown***

A strong, healthy relationship can be one of the best supports in your life. Good relationships improve all aspects of your life, your health, your mind, and your connections with others. However, if the relationship isn't working, it can also be a tremendous drain. According to HelpGuide.org, "Relationships are an investment. The more you put in, the more you can get back."

Most individuals have quite a number of

personal relationships. Relationships add quality to our lives. Since they are an integral part of who we are, it is important that we form relationships with people who can add that quality. One of the most powerful determinants of how we feel about ourselves is based on how other individuals influence us. How do we "get" the influence? We get it through our relationships, either directly or indirectly. Our most common and frequent relationships are established with family, friends, teachers, classmates, business associates, and with that special someone. How we handle or manage those relationships require commitment and skill.

Parental Relationships

The parent-child relationship is one of the longest-lasting social ties that human beings can establish. This tie is highly positive and supportive, but it also commonly includes feelings of irritation, tension, and ambivalence (Birditt, 2009). Being a parent can also be one of the most rewarding and fulfilling experiences of your life, but that doesn't mean it's easy. No matter what age a child is, a parent's work is never done. A "good" parent needs to know how to make his or her child feel valued and loved, while teaching the difference between right and wrong. At the end of the day, the most important thing is to create a nurturing environment where the child feels confident and independent. Since children are given to parents from God, both parents and children should honor the relationship. Finally, one of God's promises is directed to children: "Children, obey your parents in the Lord: for this is right. Honor thy father and mother (which is the first commandment with promise," (Ephesians 6:1-2 ASV).

Listen; age brings wisdom. Sometimes when you are young, you do not appreciate the importance of life's experiences. You can obtain knowledge very early in life, but wisdom comes from experience – living a long life.

Build a rapport with your parents; an open door

is easier to walk through than a closed one. Parents want you to share with them. They are usually willing to offer solicited or unsolicited advice. What's important is that you realize how special it is to have parents with whom you can have an open communicative relationship. In other words, parents who you can talk to, regardless of the issue.

Trust your parents (guardians); they want the best for you. Isn't it ironic that we trust our parents when we are very young, but as we mature, we find it a challenge and even difficult? Our parents want us to be independent as we enter young adulthood, but that does not mean our parents want to divorce us, desert us, or send a message that "you're on your own." Communicate with your parents; it builds trust. Building trust is reciprocal; it works both ways! Don't miss out on an amazing opportunity to continue the bond with your parents that began when you were so young.

So, if you trust your parents, should they be your best friends? I think not! They have different roles.

In fact, aren't there enough other people you know that could be your friends other than your parents? If you answered "no," would you hang out with your parents and allow them to read your Facebook and Twitter accounts like you permit your friends? Would you use the same language with your parents (who are now your best friends) that you use when you are just hanging out, frustrated, disappointed, trying to "fit in"? I think not! Need I say more?

Friends

Ancient philosophers and scientists agree: strong social ties are the KEY to happiness (Rubin, 2009). Sharing yourself with others is essential for developing meaningful relationships. I have often heard that one's net worth is the average of the friends you associate with.

Whether you are talking about your new Ipad with a friend or sharing your secrets with someone you care about deeply, both of you must agree to share personal information. It is through conversations like this that we form special relationships with people we call our “friends” – who might be male or female.

Friends enrich your life. Many of the social problems individuals face are due to the loss of family members and friends due to death, individuals moving away and job transitions. Sadly, many people experience social problems because they are lonely – they have no friends or close relationships. Friendships matter; they make a difference in the quality of our lives!

Reminders:

- ✓ Define friendship very narrowly. (For example, I have a lot of associates but fewer than a dozen true friends).
- ✓ You don’t have to speak to friends every day, and they will understand.
- ✓ You can be yourself. Won’t be judged by them. They are willing to tell you the difficult but would not do it out of malice.

- ✓ Don't get in a popularity contest- Don't try to buy friends. Don't be someone you are not, just to be in the clique.

Know how to *choose* friends:

Think you don't get to choose your friends? You get just as much say who your friends are as they do. Making friends is one thing, but choosing who your friends are is incredibly important. Your friends are your guides in life as well as the people who help define who you are. In some ways, they are family. There are some friends who are closer to you than others, but who you choose to share important parts of your life with matters (Mahoney, 2014).

Reminders:

- ✓ Determine who should be in your life and for what reason.
- ✓ Identify individuals with whom you share similar values or life paths and emulate them.

- ✓ Don't tell any one friend all of your business. Don't give any one person that much power over you.
- ✓ Don't give anyone information to hurt you.
- ✓ Build relationships based on common interests?
- ✓ Consider being a joiner. Friendships come from participating in a club, sorority, or church group. There is value in sororities and other sisterhood groups. Typically, there are chapters throughout the country which provide for immediate ways to meet individuals with common interests fairly quickly when moving to a new city.

Know when to *lose* a friend:

Some people are in your life for a season. Some friends might be tied to you when you are in high school or college and after you graduate you may not see them again. Sometimes we try to keep a person that is in your life for a season to be a friend for eternity, and that doesn’t work.

If your friends start engaging in behavior that is not acceptable to you, or don’t fit with your value system, cut them off. As an example, your friends decide to engage in drugs, bullying, gossiping, or illegal behavior, it’s time to phase out of those relationships. If they are people you like for a particular reason, and you feel compelled to stay connected, limit your time with them.

Reminders:

- ✓ Be non-responsive. Don't answer your friend's calls unless you have to.
- ✓ Quit texting. Don't text your friend and don't reply to texts. Even if you are bored, don't give your friend the wrong message by texting.
- ✓ Don’t be rude or mean. Sometimes this is difficult when you are young, and you are losing interest in someone. Try not to hurt him or her by being a bully.

Know when to *refuse* friendships:

Every relationship is not for you. If the individuals are not going in the same direction that you are, they may not be fit to be your friends. If they are dropping out of school, having children out of wedlock, disrespecting their parents and others, they may not be for you. Have courage if your friends make plans to engage in behavior you really don't want to. Be honest and say you don't want to go to that place or engage in that activity. Remember, you are not required to give an explanation.

Know how to be a *good* friend:

Being a good friend isn't always easy, but taking the time to nurture a lasting friendship is worth every ounce of effort. As the years pass, some people will stay by your side, but many won't, and you'll realize that each friendship you keep is priceless. Of course, to have a good friend, you must be one, and it takes a lot of effort and care. To be a good friend, you have to establish a trusting friendship, be there for your friend during hard times, and deepen a friendship to make it last.

Reminders:

- ✓ Don't always be on the receiving end of the friendship, always getting but not giving. Be there for others.
- ✓ Be the person others admire and want to be like.
- ✓ Stop and call or send your friends a note just to say hello.
- ✓ Don't be so busy that you can't take time out for friends. Don't go to your grave wishing you had spent more time with friends and family.
- ✓ Don't be a gossiper. If someone is gossiping about someone else to you, you can bet they are doing the same about you to someone else. Let the gossipers know that you're not interested.
- ✓ Be kind to one another.

Intimate Relationships (Male/Female Relationships, Significant Other):

Although we have friends, all friendships are not the same. Several factors determine the kind of friendship you have with another person. In early adulthood, and maybe later in life, we establish an intimate relationship with another person. Intimacy occurs on many levels. For example, in most romantic relationships, physical intimacy is a way of expressing love. However, intimacy is any form of sensual expression with another individual. Intimacy can exist in non-romantic relationships also. It occurs on emotional and intellectual levels.

Remember: Don't be defined by who you are with or whether you have someone or not. What is important is that you monitor your "special relationships," by asking yourself the following questions from time-to-time:

- ✓ Am I being treated with love and respect?
- ✓ Am I being pressured for sex or other things that I am not interested in doing?

- ✓ Am I being honest about who I think is best for me?
- ✓ Am I compromising my standards and level of respect, just to have a romantic relationship?

Demand the respect you deserve!

Dating is a special period in relationship building. It takes time and should not be rushed! Be patient! Dating should not be a "hunting" game. You and the young man should "discover" each other. Ideally, let him find you. However, you must be accessible. He is probably not going to find you if you are *always* at home. As such, make careful choices and decisions before and during the dating experience.

Dating is accompanied by having to make new and often tough decisions. Don't be afraid to express yourself; your opinion matters! Don't allow your perspectives to be stifled or ignored. The courting or dating period is like the "summer" season: Everyone is typically on his or her best behavior.

Be happy with yourself. I enjoyed being single, and now I enjoy being married. If you can find contentment with being with yourself, then you won't settle for second rate, just to have someone. Many women get concerned about the "ticking clock" and the desire to be married and have children. God knows the desires of your heart. Be patient, and let God send the right person to you.

You might ask yourself, "Where can I meet that special someone?" Consider the following:

- At work
- Through community service
- Attending planned social events
- Referrals from friends
- Singles groups at church
- Professional affiliations
- Sporting events

Reminders:

- ✓ Meet in a public place in the early dating phase.

- ✓ Be prepared to pay your share of the bill (eating out, movies, theatre, etc.)
  Expect the man to pick up the tab for the date, but as time goes by, be prepared to share in the expense and be willing to pick up the tab from time to time.
- ✓ Communicate clearly and often.

Relationship Blunders

Giving Away Joy - When you meet that special person, don't release your happiness to him. The joy that we have was not given by others, so they should not be allowed to take it away. So be careful, cherish your relationships – especially the "very special ones".

Insecurity in a relationship occurs when you think someone will take your "special man" away from you. If that is possible, then he wasn't really for you in the first place. Will it hurt and be painful? Absolutely! Think of it as God has someone better for you. Learn from every setback. Ask yourself, were you really evenly yoked? Were you friends first?

Jealousy is an action that can ruin a good relationship. Some women are insecure about their mate having female friends. Jealousy is not healthy or helpful. If the relationship is not working out, let him go! Don't smother him. If he wanders and don't come back, he wasn't yours in the first place. A guy should not be expected to spend every free moment with you. Continue to engage in other activities that are fulfilling that do not include your partner. Continue to spend time with your friends.

Tolerating Disrespect – An old adage reminds us that people treat us the way we allow them to. Expect nothing differently from your dating partner. Do not let occasional bouts of disrespect keep going unaddressed. Your mate should know what you will and won't tolerate. Respect yourself, and others will respect you.

Engaging in Sexual Relations – Sex was designed for marriage but because of worldly temptations, suggestive movies, and television programs, many single people find themselves yielding. Engaging in sex should not be viewed as “just fun.” It is a serious decision that should be made by mature adults. Don’t get caught up in the hype and falling for the line that “everybody is doing it.” Wait until the appropriate time with the appropriate person.

Reflections/Plan of Action

"Want to improve your relationships? See love as a verb rather than as a feeling." ~ **Stephen Covey**

- ✓ What relationships are most important to me? (Identify those relationships).

  ____

  ____

- ✓ What values must be present in my relationship with others?

  ____

  ____

- ✓ What am I willing to do to maintain these relationships?

  ____

  ____

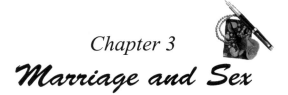

Chapter 3
Marriage and Sex

"He who finds a wife finds what is good and receives favor from the Lord."
Proverbs 18:22 NIV

"In my mind, marriage is a spiritual partnership and union in which we willingly give and receive love, create and share intimacy, and open ourselves to be available and accessible to another human being in order to heal, learn and grow."
~ Iyanla Vanzant

Genesis, Chapters 1 and 2, reflect that God created man (Adam) and decided that he needed a mate. So God created Eve, because He did not want Adam to be alone - thus, the beginning of relationships. Many individuals view marriage as a public expression of their love for another, and for centuries, matrimony has been a very public institution impacted by tradition, culture, religion, and laws. Throughout centuries, the institution of marriage has been changing and continues to change (About.com/marriage). However, one fact has not changed: God designed marriage and has a plan for it. In order for a marriage to work the way God designed it, a man and a woman must be obedient to God's plan for marriage and His Word.

Finding that special someone – that man you want to spend the rest of your life with -- is often a task, maybe even a challenge. For many chores or tasks, we tend to be self-sufficient, (i.e. we can do chores and tasks ourselves or know how to hire help). This "task" – if that's your perspective on finding a mate – lies with you. Don't expect someone to select that special someone for you. You need to make that decision for yourself!

Mr. Right will want you for you! Don't rush into marriage; make sure you are equally yoked (have similar interests or values). With God guiding you, you can make a well-informed decision.

Once married, be committed to your vows. The following vows are commonly used during the ceremony: *For better, for worse, for richer, for poorer, in sickness and in health, to love and to cherish, till death do us part…* If you go into the marriage with the understanding that divorce is not an option, you are proned to work harder to make the marriage work. You can't do that if the union was not put together by God.

If God puts you and your mate together, you will experience joy and happiness in the marriage. However, don't rely on your joy and happiness to come from your mate. Have your own unspeakable joy. It is important to love yourself first.

Many couples expect their mate to be perfect in the marriage. Don't expect perfection from your mate because you are not perfect either. Don't be blinded by fairy tales. The reality of marriage is that it takes work from each mate. The first few years is the honeymoon period where we are infatuated with the institution of marriage. Love will have a different meaning after the honeymoon period. It will be sustained by mutual respect and effective communication.

Communication is critical for a successful marriage! Let your mate know what makes you happy and what disappoints you or makes you sad. Don't leave it up to your mate to guess what's going on with you. Marriage is serious; it is not a game. You can maintain mutual respect, if you have your priorities in order. Know your priorities: God, husband/wife, children, family, and friends = God ordained order.

You and your mate will bring family and friends into the marriage. Have a clear understanding about the role that your friends will have, especially friends of the opposite sex. Be careful not to put other men in the role of your mate, allowing them to fill in where there is a deficit.

A successful marriage requires falling in love many times, always with the same person (McLaughlin, 2001). Marriage is about commitment, sacrifice, and compromise. The most successful marriages put God first.

God designed marriage for a man and a woman. An expression of the love between the two is demonstrated through sex. A husband and a wife should fulfill each other's sexual needs. In marriage, nothing is taboo. Since God ordained marriage, He supports and blesses the union between husband and wife.

Make sure the young man chooses you! The Bible says in Proverbs 18:22 (NIV), "He who finds a wife finds what is good and receives favor from the Lord." You are to be treated like God treated the church. Contrary to popular belief in many circles, chivalry is not dead. Don't be embarrassed when a young man treats you like God wants you to be treated. Your husband should love and treat you as an act of service unto God. After all, a wife is a gift from God! Don't tolerate any abuse, physical or verbal. Words hurt more and can cut deeper than physical wounds.

Make sure you are in love and just not infatuated with your mate. Taking the time to get to know your mate is important. Having that time, allows you to notice red flags or warning signs. You must be willing to ask the right questions and listen to the answers. Many people are not willing or patient enough to take the time to get to know their significant other prior to marriage, even though a number of differences abound! You are better off spending the necessary time to invest in your relationship than ignoring the warning signs.

Don't expect that you will be able to change your husband after you get married. What you see, is what you get! Don't be fooled by the notion that you can change someone after you are in a committed relationship or get married. That is nothing but pure fantasy. People can change, but it is their decision, not yours! Listen to your intuition. Let it guide you. You may be surprised!

Check out his relationships with the women in his life: his mother, sisters and female friends. Some of you may have heard that how a man treats his mother and sister(s) is an indication of how he will treat you – his wife. Certainly, life has no guarantees, but observing your significant other's behavior toward these special females – with whom you would expect he adores - should not be ignored.

Marriage is a big step! For this reason, having the tough conversations prior to marriage is critical. Some of the topics can be easily swept under the rug, while others are common and frequently discussed between two individuals heading toward the altar. Prior to marriage, talk about finances, children, returning to school, and home ownership – early and often. These topics are easily avoided, because some people don't know how to discuss them – or don't like to. Others avoid discussing them, because they don't understand the repercussions of delaying the conversations. Don't procrastinate!

Reflections/Plan of Action

"Love is partnership of two unique people who bring out the very best in each other, and who know that even though they are wonderful as individuals, they are even better together." ~ **Barbara Cage**

- ✓ One should have more reasons to get married than not to get married. What are 3-4 reasons to get married?

  ____

  ____

- ✓ What are 3-4 reasons not to get married?

  ____

  ____

- ✓ Does your mate have similar values and goals for life?

  ____

  ____

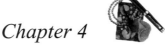

Chapter 4
Taking Care of Your Spiritual and Emotional Health

"He heals the brokenhearted and binds up their wounds [curing their pains and their sorrows]."
Psalms 147:3 AMP

"We are stronger than we think...We may get knocked down, but we don't have to stay down."
~ Steve Goodier

Most of us are aware of people who are addicted to some type of substance, whether it is food, alcohol, drugs, sex, etc. We also hear on a regular basis about someone trying to commit suicide: perhaps you know someone personally. Why is this occurring? I suspect it is because they are having difficulty coping with some negative emotion. There is so much that can be said about how to cope - too much for just one chapter. It is my hope that you understand the influence of any positive or negative emotion you may experience - then accept these tips on how to overcome the negative emotions and practice focusing on the positive ones.

We must win the battle over negative emotions because negative emotions have a direct correlation to our physical well-being. Not coping with negative emotions can cause stress that can lead to a multitude of physical ailments, including high blood pressure or a stroke. These emotions can result in insomnia, obesity, addictions and more. They are not only dangerous but could be life-threatening.

So what are these negative emotions? Depending on how you define them, there could be a long list but I just want to focus on 10 that I call *potentially deadly emotions*. They are anger, bitterness, depression, fear, grief, guilt, hatred, jealousy, shame, and worry. It's not a matter of IF you will experience any, or all of these "emotions," but WHEN. Will you have the arsenal in your tool kit to overcome them when they occur? As I explain the 10 negative emotions, I share some suggestions on how to cope with them.

Negative Emotions

Anger - the hostile feeling you might have against someone (family member, friend, significant other, boss, etc.) because they hurt you, consciously or unconsciously.

At some point, you will have to let the anger go as something of your past and not of your present; forgive those who have hurt you whether they feel remorse or not. Anger doesn't hurt the person we feel anger toward as much as it does us. It can eat you up on the inside, so we must learn to release it.

Bitterness – emotion, sometimes described as resentment, presents itself because someone has wronged you in some way.
Like coping with anger, don't dwell on the action, but forgive and move forward.

Depression - feeling dejected, low spirits.
Do something for others; surround yourself with positive people.

Fear - anxiety over real or perceived danger to your well-being.
Face up to it; Believe Isaiah 54:17- "No weapon form against you shall prosper."

Grief - intense emotional suffering caused by a loss.
Allow yourself time to heal and manage the pain of the loss; Seek trusted individuals with whom to share your feelings.

Guilt - feeling of regret based on doing something wrong or hurtful.
Acknowledge you were wrong; Forgive yourself; accept the consequences of your actions; ask for forgiveness from the other party.

Hatred - a strong dislike for someone.
Recognize there is no benefit for carrying this feeling about anyone. Again, it doesn't hurt the person as much as it consumes the energy that can be used for more positive actions.

Jealousy - envious of others; desirous of what others have.
Understand what is for you, is for you.

Shame - guilt for wrongdoing.
Forgive yourself and learn from your mistakes.

Worry - a troubled state of mind; to agonize over something real or imagined.
"Pray and if you are going to pray, don't worry. If you are going to worry, don't pray." In other words, pray and then release it. Consider assessing the alternatives and derive a solution. Think through what would be the worst thing that could happen, and then determine what you will do in that situation, then release it. You take the mystery out of it.

Overcoming Negative Emotions

We turn negative emotions around through a positive attitude that is shaped by our thoughts, our words, and ultimately, our actions. What can help mold our positive attitude? I offer the following:

Surround yourself with positive, upbeat people – These are people who look at a glass as half full rather than half empty. Individuals who, through their words and actions, support and believe in you.

Listen to upbeat music – Music can impact your mood – especially upbeat music! People are usually happier when they listen to up tempo music. Try it!

Laugh - Laughter is still good for the soul and has been said to be the best medicine.

Positive affirmations – Encourage yourself by posting positive phrases where they are readily seen by you; on your bathroom mirror, in your car, on your desk at work, etc. This exercise is an effective way to boost your spirits and build self-esteem.

Tears are the relief valve for the heart – Crying is healthy and is an opportunity for an emotional release. Tears help you clear "stuff" out of your system. Without tears, life would be too uptight!

Positive Emotions

Psychologist Barbara Frederickson, in her book *Positivity*, presents the results of more than 20 years of investigating positive emotions. She says these emotions can make us healthier and happier if we take the time to cultivate them. Negative emotions occur more naturally through everyday life. The secret is to balance the negative by increasing the positive emotions. In doing so, you find a more meaningful and clearer purpose in life, have fewer health issues and more positive personal relationships. So here are those 10 most common positive emotions:

Amusement - The emotion that makes you smile or laugh occurs when you are in a playful, humorous situation with others (i.e. laughing at a funny joke, participating in a fun activity).

Awe – The feeling of reverence, admiration, or wonder you have for someone or something. Some of my favorites are the waves of the Atlantic Ocean from the sandy beaches, a beautiful sunset, or the vast mountains of Arizona. They all remind me of the awesomeness of our Creator.

Gratitude - The feeling of appreciation and thankfulness for something you have received.

Hope – The feeling or expectation that my desired outcome will happen.

Inspiration - A feeling or a stimulus to a creative thought or action. For me, when someone excels beyond the ordinary, it motivates me to act beyond my own ordinary. An example would be an athlete in the Special Olympics or an individual who despite their poor economic circumstances excels academically or professionally.

Interest – The feeling of curiosity or concern about something. It is a state of intrigue where you want to know more. It compels you to be open to new experiences and have a desire to explore the world around you. After visiting a foreign country, I was compelled to learn more about the norms and customs of that culture.

Joy – The feeling of happiness, a positive and memorable experience you've had. For me, this is the unspeakable joy that I feel that the world didn't give me and the world can't take it away.

Love – The feeling of affection and personal attachment for something or someone.

Pride – A high opinion of oneself for having accomplished a feat.

Serenity – A feeling of calm and peacefulness. This is a time when I can sit back and relax without a worry in the world; a time where I can be in the moment, no worrying about the past and no anticipation about the future.

These positive emotions are a reaction to your current circumstances. Just as you can see the negative in your circumstances, it is possible to see the good or the positive as well. You have to choose to do so.

Spiritual Health

I want to close this chapter by talking about spiritual health. God promises that He will be with us always! However, He left us with the opportunity of free will – to make our own choice(s). We are at liberty to make choices and live with the consequences of those choices. God won't keep us from falling into the jaws of the evil one, if we choose to, but He shows us the way out. Continue to listen to the small, still voice. Sometimes God speaks to me through others, validating what the Holy Spirit has told me.

Many of us have been introduced to church, to religion, but not spirituality. Spirituality is our connection with God and allowing that relationship to guide our daily lives. In the words of Lasana Omar Hotep, "Think of religion as a vehicle and spirituality as the destination." Trust and be assured that God has a plan for your life! I thought when I dedicated my life to God's plan, everyday would be like a holiday! Not!! But without accepting his direction is like going on a trip to a new destination without a map.

Considerations

- ✓ Prioritize your faith – Put God first, then others things will be added unto you. Trust in the Lord, and lean not to your own understanding.
- ✓ Practice your faith – Live your life based on biblical principles (pray, meditate, attend worship services, and tithe). It is important to live your faith 24/7 and not just on your day of worship.
    - Pray – Pray without ceasing; prayer changes things!
    - Worship – Find a church or a spiritual place where you feel the Holy Spirit. Attending church gives me the strength to ward off the challenges of the world for the week.
- ✓ Promote your faith – Actions speak louder than words! Many times, you may be the

only Bible or church others may experience. God wants us to show what He is all about through our behavior/actions.

- ✓ Learn to forgive yourself – There is nothing we can do that will make God stop loving us. He has unconditional love and will love us no matter what! God knows what we are going to do before we do it, and the Bible reminds us that God knew us in our mother's womb. He even knows every hair on our head.

Pastor Kerwin Brown states, "You cannot promote what you don't practice and you don't practice what you don't prioritize." With that in mind, make your spiritual health a priority.

Take care of your spiritual and emotional health! Doing so can lead to a clearer life purpose, better personal relationships, and enhanced stress management skills (Mayo Clinic Staff, 2014).

Reflections/Plan of Action

"It is not possible to be spiritually mature while remaining emotionally immature."

~ Peter Scazzero

- ✓ What does spiritual health mean to me?

  ____

  ____

- ✓ Am I balancing negative emotions with positive emotions? Explain your response.

  ____

  ____

- ✓ What are my next steps to improve my spiritual and emotional health?

  ____

  ____

Chapter 5
Taking Care of Your Physical Health

"Therefore, I urge you, brothers, in view of God's mercy, to offer your bodies, as living sacrifices, holy and pleasing to God – this is your spiritual act of worship."

Romans 12:1 NIV

"Take care of your body. It's the only place you have to live."

~ Jim Rohn

We must love ourselves enough to take care of ourselves. Our body is a temple from God, and I believe it is our responsibility to take the best care of it. Your goal should be to have a physically fit body and lifestyle. This is a very personal decision and should not be taken lightly. You owe it to yourself and everyone who cares about you to be as physically fit as possible in order to have a productive life. I offer the following suggestions for your consideration:

- ✓ **Annual physical exam** - Knowledge is power! Having a regular check-up is the only way to ensure your body is functioning properly. Many medical conditions can be addressed successfully, if diagnosed early. With the guidance of your physician, you will know your ideal weight and body mass.
- ✓ **Eat in moderation** – Have several small meals throughout the day. Breakfast is the most important meal! Eat fresh fruits and vegetables. Be mindful of your intake of fat, sugar, and sodium.
- ✓ **Drink plenty of water** – Our bodies need plenty of water! Many of us tend not to drink enough water. Drinking 6-8 glasses of water daily is suggested by medical and health professionals. To make water more palatable, consider adding fruit, cucumbers, or non-alcoholic drink mixes.

- ✓ **Consistent sleep** – Make it a point to get 6-8 hours of sleep regularly. Few of us get enough sleep and lack of sleep impacts our metabolism, mental capacity and overall wellness. It's not a good idea to sleep less during the week, while sleeping longer hours on the weekend. Attempt to stay consistent.
- ✓ **Exercise regularly** – Ouch!! Yes, it is very important that we spend an average of 30 minutes daily on physical activity. Find an activity or activities that you enjoy. A physical trainer was asked once which exercises would benefit a person the most. He answered, "[The] ones that you will do." It could be a brisk walk, dancing to your favorite tunes or working out in the gym – it's your call. Exercise is one of the best ways to ensure you live a long, healthy and productive life. Exercise increases stamina, mental sharpness, and resistance to illnesses.

- ✓ **Eliminate stressors** – Stressors can impact your physical health, so try to reduce or avoid your exposure to them. This might include negative people, procrastination, or trying to live up to other people's expectations or standards.
- ✓ **Reduce or eliminate controlled substances** – If we remember that our body is our temple, then we are not likely to engage in smoking, drinking or recreational drugs. We know the use of these vices are detrimental to our overall well-being. Whatever problems you are trying to escape by binging on food, drinking or shooting-up on drugs, they will still be there when you "come off the high."
- ✓ **Appearance** – Why is there so much attention about how someone looks? What difference does it make if an individual is not dressed the way someone else might expect? It matters a lot! Is this fair? No, but fair or not, it's life! We are judged based on our first

impression. We have choices to conform or not. We just have to be prepared to accept the consequences of our actions.

It matters how a young lady presents herself in public. Your appearance communicates more than you might think. With this in mind, make sure you are presenting a positive image and an image of which you are most proud; first impressions are lasting! If you are in doubt about what appearance is appropriate, observe other women in the circle you aspire to be in.

As you make this determination, I offer the following considerations:

- Hair – clean and well-groomed
- Makeup – appropriate for the occasion
- Clothing - Don't invest a lot of money in the latest fads; they phase out quickly.

Invest in basic pieces of attire that can be worn over the years. Wear patterns and fabrics that complement your body shape – not detract from it.

Reflections/Plan of Action

- ✓ What one area of my physical self do I need to improve? How will I do it?

  ____

  ____

- ✓ What is one activity that I will stop, start, or continue in order to maintain a better physical appearance?

  ____

  ____

- ✓ Who is the person(s) I admire that appear to be physically healthy? What can I learn from them that I can apply to improving my physical health?

  ____

  ____

Chapter 6
Finance: Economic Empowerment

"Money, like emotions, is something you must control to keep your life on the right track."
~ **Natasha Munson**

Your money is a huge part of your life. It can determine what you can do and where you can go. Learning how to manage your money the right way is an important step toward taking control of your life. Understand where your money is coming from, where it's going to, and how to make sure that the way you manage your money falls in line with the values that matter most to you.

Managing Money

Budget – A realistic budget is the most important component of your financial plan. I remember reading that 60% of America is spending money that they earn every month and beyond because they have not learned the practice of budgeting. You need to start practicing early in life to "save for a rainy day."

Credit Card Debt – The purpose of credit cards should be to 1) establish and maintain credit history; and 2) give extra financial protection in case of an emergency. You should never spend money on your credit cards that you are not prepared to pay back immediately or when due. You should not use the card for everyday purchases; use debit cards for that purpose. Debit card purchases are deducted from your checking account balance right away. Eliminate all credit cards balances as soon as possible.

A FICO score is used to determine your credit worthiness. In other words, this score determines if you get a favorable interest rate on credit cards, car loans, apartment leases, mortgages, and even consideration for employment – especially if you will be responsible for handing money. If you are in a career where you influence financial decisions and your financial portfolio is not stable, you may be considered a financial risk to the organization.

A FICO score of 680 -719 is a good score and an excellent credit score is 720 and above.

According to most credit counselors, five factors impact your FICO score:

- Timely payments of bills and other financial obligations
- Length of credit history
- Debt-to-loan ratios (balance on credit cards and other loans compared to your total credit limit)
- Recent loan applications, current inquiries, and new accounts
- Mixture of credit cards and loans.

Be sure to check your FICO score regularly. You can do this by obtaining your credit report. Various credit card companies reflect your score on your monthly billing statements. Be aware that on average 75% of all credit reports reflect errors. You are allowed to obtain one free report per year from each credit reporting bureau: Equifax, Experian, and TransUnion. Obtain and download your reports by using the following link www.annualcreditreport.com

Saving Money

Prepare an Emergency Fund - It is vital to have 3-6 months of living expenses saved in case of an emergency. On average, if you are out of work, it could take 6 months to a year to find a job. Therefore, it is imperative to have funds you can access fairly easily.

Real Estate – Home ownership is one of your first levels of investing. Never purchase a home that requires more than twice the total household income. Know how much you can afford *before* looking for a new home. It can be awfully frustrating and embarrassing to fall in love with a home that you cannot afford.

Life Insurance – Purchase life insurance and have a well-written policy so if you are faced with a life-changing event with a death of a loved one, you will be prepared financially to handle it.

Stocks and Bonds – These financial tools are the most common vehicles where you can invest your money. Acquire professional services from a reputable financial planner who can provide sound investment advice and counseling.

Wills and Trust (Save from Probate) – One most commonly asked question dealing with finance is: Do I need a will? The answer is: It depends. If you want your *expressed* intentions known after your death regarding your possessions, the answer is yes! You should have a will created as soon as you acquire possessions (anything of importance to you). You don't know what tomorrow may bring, so prepare and spare your survivors and friends the agony of trying to figure out what you wanted to do with your "things." You may opt to have the will created legally by an attorney or draft your own.

If your intentions are not clearly communicated in the will regarding larger possessions like property, those unanswered questions will be resolved in probate court. Probate ensures that your final business is handled legally.

Making Money

Career – Your job will probably be your primary source of income. For this reason, decide on a career early in your professional life. A job is a source of income and provides a regular check; however, you want to build a career. A career will provide job stability, professional development, and a source of income for retirement.

Entrepreneur – Self-employed individuals have more control over their professional lives because they work for themselves. However, they are also held accountable to the people for whom they provide products and services. If you decide to pursue this path, make sure you develop a business plan, have passion and skills for the profession, and have an insatiable desire to succeed! Assess from time to time if you are "fit" for this kind of work. You have to believe that no one else can do this job better than you!

Reflections/Plan of Action

"Earn nicely!!! Spend wisely!! Live happily!!

~ ***Auliq Ice***

- ✓ What does managing money mean to me?

  ____

  ____

- ✓ Do I have a plan to manage my money now? If so, how?

  ____

  ____

- ✓ What are my financial goals?

  ____

  ____

In Closing...

The lessons shared are not new, but I offer them from my personal life experiences. As with many successful persons, I stand on the shoulders of many who came before me and were willing to coach or mentor me over the years. To all of you, too numerous to mention by name, I say thank you for all the invaluable advice and counsel. In addition to my mentors, I have gained knowledge from workshops, conferences and lectures I have attended, as well as books I have read. Where I have remembered, I have referenced cited sources. In other cases, I shared how I applied their principles to my life.

So, what are you going to do now with the information in this book? It is my prayer that you will move from *where you are* to a little closer to *where you want to be*. As you continue on your journey, revisit "Lessons..." from time to time. You have made it this far; you can keep moving! The only difference is that now you have more information than you had before you read this book. Use the information! I said at the beginning that this book is for you, and it is! Own it! As you are starting the first day of the rest of your life, and you are creating your roadmap, consider the following questions:

1. What is the take-away message for you from each chapter?
2. Which chapter/section touched your spirit the most?
3. To what extent have you put any of these "lessons" into practice?
4. Will you "Pay it Forward" by sharing any of the lessons with others?
5. What goals have you set for yourself for the next month? Six months? Year?

As you put these "lessons" into practice, I ask that you recite the *Serenity Prayer* (Reinhold Niebuhr, 1930s – originally untitled) when you come to a crossroad:

"Lord, grant me the serenity to accept the things I cannot change, the courage to change the things I can, and the wisdom to know the difference."

You do not have to be religious to allow this prayer to light your pathway. You may be reminded of it daily, weekly, monthly, or less frequently. Whenever you need it, whisper it into your spirit! So what are you waiting for? If you are ready to move *from where you are to where you want to be*, all you have to do is ACT! What better time to get started than NOW! Peace and Blessings!

About the Author

Linda Groomes Walton, author, consultant, certified life coach and adjunct professor. Founder and president of Achieving My Purpose, Inc. (AMP). She founded AMP in 2013 to establish a vehicle to pursue her passion of working with and supporting women through their life's purpose.

Previous to AMP, Ms. Walton demonstrated her leadership skills in the public and private sectors. She started her career with Hallmark Cards, led an international management consulting firm, LGC Enterprises, and worked for the City of Scottsdale (AZ) as a Human Resources and Economic Development professional.

LGC Enterprises established itself as an international management consulting firm, specializing in the area of diversity. With clients throughout the United States, Ms. Walton also conducted training globally, including the United Kingdom, Germany, Japan and Italy.

As a community servant, Ms. Walton serves as International Chair of Leadership Training for Alpha Kappa Alpha Sorority, Inc; President of the Phoenix Chapter of Links; and a Scottsdale Leadership alumnus of Class 26, where she serves on the Outreach and Recruitment committee.

Academically, Ms. Walton is a doctoral candidate in psychology at Grand Canyon University (AZ). She holds a Master of Business Administration degree in Finance from Indiana University; a Bachelor of Science Degree from Florida State University and holds a Certificate of Continuing Education from the Tuck School of Business Executive Program..

It is through her leadership, professional, community and life experiences that she is offering guidance in this book.

Lessons Learned